A Poet's Song

The Dogwood Tree And Other Poems

By

Joy Ward Davis

A Passionately Fair Publisher

Manuscript formatting, cover designing,
Interior artwork designed
By
Pat Simpson
www.apfpublisher.com

ISBN: 978-1-387-14684-0

Foreword
(Joy Ward Davis 2017)

The year was 1995. The place; a local library to get library cards for my children and myself. The lady behind the counter....became my Sister in Spirit. Having Joy in my life means much to me....we have shared many tears of sorrow and tears of great joy (All pun intended). We have lived through great events and survived through life's crisis'. Joy is someone that has risen to the top when confronted with life changing decisions. I am very proud to have Joy as a Dear Lady and Friend...she has a personal strength that others can benefit from.

You hold in your hand Joy's first book *A Poet's Song(2017) it* shows a reflection of the soul that is the core of all Joy is. All her love is poured onto these pages....her words will strike a chord and harmonize with any soul who picks up and reads this book and feels with their hearts.

Her daughter, Mary-Catherine is also featured within these pages. Her skills are wonderfully refreshing. Her gems....glitter in colors....I am so happy that Mother and Daughter have such a wonderful bond and share their love of words within these pages.

Joy's faith and her family memories are all contained in a neat package tied with a pretty bow. Each gem she lays before your lap. All you have to do....is open the book....and let the pure joy leap from these pages straight into your heart.

Joy was also the inspiration for a charity book *Cause for Paws* (2014). (http://www.lulu.com/shop/joy-davis-and-alliance-poets-world-wide/cause-for-paws/paperback/product-21792796.html published by Patricia Farnsworth-Simpson apfpublisher@gmail.com]) The proceeds from the sale of Cause for Paws benefit the many domestic animals in shelters such as Petsmart™ Charities and Scotland County Humane Society™.

Joy has a heart bigger than her body...
We will always be....Sisters...in Spirit....
We both have ink for blood and will always be at the ready....pen in hand....

Here's to you, Gentle Reader...it's time to kick back and enjoy...a most wonderful book....

© Dena M. Ferrari

Contents

Contents

Contents

Contents

Contents

Contents

Dedication

This book is dedicated to

My Daughter

Mary-Catherine

Who is my Everything

I love you Mom

Joy

Acknowledgements

This book would have never had come to be if it weren't for the following, Most of all to God for without him there would have never been a me and I surely would not still be here. To my parents, and sister, My mom Mary Ellen Chaffman Ward who encouraged me at the young age of seven writing my "first Book" and wanted to get it published even though it was Christmas eve.

My dad Phillip Ward who believe I could do anything and was proud of me no matter what.

My sister Phyllis Ward Guinn being my cheerleader always there for me cheering me on and believing in me. I know you are all looking down on me beaming with happiness. Know I love and miss you. Rest In Peace.
To two special Aunts, Carol Tracy and Pearl Graham you have been an inspiration to my life, being there, listening and always believing in me.

To my Transcending church family and friends who showed me not to quit to always move forward and always believe God is with us.

My friends through the years past and current you are a special part of my heart because you stuck by me and knew one day this book would happen for your loyalty, your trust and your love it means the world to me Thank you for embracing my life. CarolB, Cindy, Lisa , Jill , Tammy, Sherry, Anita, Pattye Doris , Janet, Carol ,Debbie , Dale, Melanie, Lee, James Jim, Leroy, DavidM and if any I missed who were on my path in life. Know I love and appreciate you. Thank You!

To Pat Farnworth-Simpson of AFP Publishers a huge Thank you for this opportunity a dream come true for me. For the Writer's and Poetry Alliance introduced to me by Dena has been truly a Godsent to my life an outlet that has been awesome in all the poets I have met there and the common bond we share putting words to paper for all to enjoy. A Poet's Song is my message, My "song" and contains poems also by my daughter Mary-Catherine and a poem written together by Dena Ferrari another poet and dear friend. Thank You.

JOY

A Poet's Song

Words on paper

are the notes in

my song sung

together into a

special rhyme

to live on

to be sung

many times.

Joy

Dogwood Tree

Tall slender
softly tanned
sways
to the music of the wind
like a ballerina
dancing on a dark stage
reaching for the impossible
gracefully ending
in a stillness of beauty.

Silence

In the stillness of the night
before the darkness falls
silence creeps in on me
the night grows near
it embraces me
silence rocks me
and soothes my soul
like a mother who hushes
her child to sleep.

Solidness

Seagrove NC

The Essence of the
Molding Form
Handed down through
Generations
Family rooted in the
Solidness of the tradition
Hard like clay
Lasting Forever

Dear Child of Mine
For Mary-Catherine

Dear Child of Mine
We waited so long
for You
Finally You are here
Our little angel
embracing our Lives
with a Love so overwhelming
it leaves our heart bursting
Every day is a new experience
Looking at the world through
Your eyes

Brings such joy to our days
Showing you our world
Makes everything more exciting
As time moves on
We promise to continue to
Enrich your life
with all that we can
As you have enriched our
Just by being in Our Midst.

4

Cousins

There were four of us

cousins growing up

with city lights and row houses

catching lightening bugs

being together is what made

it special and fun

a tree a shore

a Mimi's love

Mom's always there

shown us that memories are real

and we hung onto them

even when

cousins grow up and life changes

miles between us now

children cousins of their own

continue on making memories

living on today and always.

Black

Black is space and the dark sky
black is the color of a black cat
who people are afraid of
black is mascara
when you put it on
boys think it's hot
black is a trash bag
empty or full

© Mary-Catherine Davis

Do We Even Know

Our heart when its
shattered scars
hardly covering the
wounds
Do we even know
how it feels
trying to put the
pieces in place
where they been ripped
and torn
Do we even know
if there are any
chances left
for our heart
to feel the pulse
beating
once more
never really knowing
if we even know
how it feels
if our heart
can embrace
again...

Historic Stagville

House on the Hill
Forgotten it seems
For all to see
Lands around it
Homes to many
Once upon a time
Master to Slave
Much work to do
Generations
Living through
Hard times indeed
Finding their way
As each day passes
Into the night
Loving living Land
Their only right
Spirit willing
Life lives on
In the memories
Of an Antebellum
Plantation.

Soldier Boy

Little soldier boy
from the West Virginia mountains
serving his country out from
coal mine country
he was small but he done
a lot in life
now there was still more to
do and see
leaving his love behind
to places he never imagined
seeing but love of life,
his country and Nancy
made it worth it
Little soldier boy came back home
but many lives lost he seen
he never forgotten them
they live on in his heart today

as he watches his grandson
soldier boy becomes a man
his heart burst with love
as he remembers and never
forgets those soldier boys
long ago
and remembers them now
in his grandson of today.

* In Honor of MCKinnley Graham served 1960-1983

That Dirt Road Home

There were five of us
that grew up on that dirt Road
we called Home
where parents still hollered out
for us kids to come in
where we ran and played
till the wee hours having fun
the way it should be
watching stars twinkle down
at us as they knew all our secrets
we thought they did but who knows
we never tell
the girl with the golden hair, the dainty girl,
little girl who followed the rest of us
trying to fit in, the middle cousin and Me
five girls growing up on that dirt road
Life was simple back then just walk
to the store and get candy, a drink
sunflower seeds play for hours in a pool
then freeze when you went inside
annoying brothers Buck and Joe
spying on us

we were Charlie's Angels and
girls only clubhouse
reading books checked out from
Joy's library
kool aid and moon pies we sneaked
to have our own fun time
living on that dirt road
no worries or cares
summer was fun because we had each other
and that's what mattered most of All.

In Honor of Jill, Tammy, Tessy, Sherry and Me

The "Cool" Uncle

I remember
in my childhood
growing up
with you around
you were cool
you always understood
us kids
got down to our level
to talk to us not at us
I remember
you made me feel special
called me Joy Ellen
and as I got older
still found time
to show I mattered
helping me with math
and my resume
like I was one of
your own
because it mattered
now your great niece
thinks your are sooo cool too
when I ask her who is her
favorite uncle etc
I not surprise when she
says old dad as she
calls you and as I ask
why because he is so cool

and memories flow back
as I remember
and I smile yeah
he is mine too
thanks for being
who you are
because we think
you are great
and for giving us
wonderful memories
Happy Birthday
Old Dad/Uncle Jim!
Love You!

* IN MEMORY OF JAMES TRACY 1939-2013 RIP

14

The Long Road

Long arms and legs
keep walking down
dirt roads
heading to town
he knows his mission
he knows the way
as chocolate colored arms
sway with each step
he takes
His sister traveled
different roads
mostly trains
that took her
far away from
their homeplace
their family of 18
knew she would be
the one to make it
and in time
she did

while he walks
the long road
that will take
him to his future
Many Generations
later
Celebrate Time
Place and a Sister
but he never
forgets who he is
even as others
now walk that
long road
to remember him
today

*In Memory of William Thomas Mcleod and the sister who
went before him making a place for their name.
Mary Mcleod Bethune.

Winter

Cold feet patter across the rug

to the warmth of the fire

glowing in the fireplace

sounds of football

blaring on the TV

while water boils on the stove

the whiteness of snow falls outside

covering the world like sugar

cold stillness of the night

the warmth of the fire

makes you dream

of roasting hotdogs

eating ice cream cones

and wishing summer was here.

Another Day

The sun bids Good Morning as it creeps across
a sky the color of the ocean blue
it bids hello to birds flying through its
shadows as they seek food
to nourish their young
Just another day opens the window
to nature in its truest form
winds embrace leaves
fly trying to catch
each other
Another day watches
all that surrounds
its soul beats wildly
enjoying all that is to be
on this just another day
Alive.

What a View

Time turns no stone

space sheds no tears

walk together

finds a way reaching

clocking ticking through the hours,

Minutes, seconds

another day

shows a way reaching to the high plateau

daring the risk

the view breath taking.

weary travelers but oh

again what a view!

Senseless

Life cut short

in the power

of blows

too powerful to stop

no control left

senseless

never ending

pounding away

at the soul

the last punch

lifeless...

Anne Frank

Anne Frank
girl of WW2
diary of her thoughts
made famous
died young 15
lives on forever
With Mary-Catherine Davis

Death

Fingers grab
Each breath
Holding tightly
Then release
Life ceases to be.

Family Tree

Solid strong trunk
with lean branches
reaches out toward
the world
like a man and woman
guiding their children
in the right way
to be their own person
generations

Wagram's Scottish Home

The year was 1813
a Scottish bride
came to America
to a small town that now
bears a German name
Wagram among its
Scottish settlers
Her name was Catherine
married to a Daniel
a preacher man
who rose above
the tribulations of the time.
They were a strong couple
faithful to the God above
who giving them life and love
by a river in this southern town
raised their children and their grand
many descendents live abound
Lawyers, authors, teachers, preachers
came from their line
A church still stands in the memory
living on today.
Remembering them All

Joy

* In honor and memory of Daniel and Catherine Campbell White
founding pastor of Spring Hill Baptist Church, Wagram, NC

Black Mountain

In the highest hills

they gathered

and all creative flows

came together

in many forms

they saw what

it is like to

be free

to be the artist

the never ending dreamer

daring to live the dream.

*In memory and honor of the Black Mountain
Poets and Artists at Black Mountain College.
1933-1957.

A Fathers Love

A Father's Love comes through in
not only hugs and kisses
Little girls learn their words of wisdom
if they will listen
My fathers voice spoke wisely
in you will have these things or
Down the road they are doing a many a thing
but that don't mean you need to do it
he showed his love in many ways
always making sure we had all of
our needs and some of our wants
my father often told me he loved me
stuck around to raise two daughters
when his wife died
but he never complained and he always
knew we needed him

He was one of the good guys
and I am proud he was mine
I say his words of wisdom often now
cause I know they were the truth
and because I know he is looking down
from heaven grinning as I am finding
it all out that he was right all along
and especially today and as all days I
remember him for like my
heavenly father he was always there
for me and today He still is
embracing our lives even more.

*IN MEMORY OF PHILLIP WARD 1929-2005

Time

I held Time in my hand today
If only for a minute
It seem to seize the moment
As the world became so still
The hurrying, the hustle of
Everyday life seem to give up
Without a fight
Time remain still till I set
It free then as quickly as it stopped
Time caught up with Me.

Time flew out the window
into an endless sky
not wanting to wait on me
Time chose to leave my side
I felt like it was goodbye

I sat waited and wondered
just what I was to do
until the sun passed into
another day
and Time returned to me

Time embraced me
like the rush of the wind
on a cloudless day
each brush of its breath
showed me
the way toward my goal
out of sight
Time brings me closer
to its grasp
so that I can know its presence.

Because we are Sisters
For Phyllis

The paths of life didn't always go
the way we thought it would
but because we are sisters
we somehow managed to
get through the rough roads we traveled
The choices we made weren't
always the ones we wanted
but through the years
we adapted to the changes
that were tossed our way
sometimes never knowing
how things would turn out to be

But because we are sisters
I knew you were always there for me
as I am here for you
as we continue on this
journey of life
it can only get better
and I am glad to have
been along for the ride.

Joy

* In Memory of my favorite and only sister
Phyllis Ward Guinn 1957-2009 RIP

Once Upon a Time

Once upon a time children played
ring around the rosy cowboys and Indians
with make believe guns
their world was peaceful
not full of guns shooting
interupting their morning
their world was full
of new things and playful days
not some madman bursting into their school
making a mess and changing
their world forever
Once upon a time stories were told
of fairy princesses going to sleep
and being kissed by their prince
not precious children
dying never to wake up again
May they never be forgotten
always living on in our hearts
even with the stories of their terror
told again and again
Lives cut too short
precious angels in heaven
they are now singing
for God. safe in his embrace
Good night...

* In Memory of the 20 children killed in Newtown, Conn.

In Memory of Grandpa

His face lined with wrinkles
showed many years of hardship
but his many words of wisdom
had many stories to tell
he told of the days of his day
when people laughed and
enjoyed the simple things
he says those were the
better days
and I believe him
He's gone now but
his many words of wisdom
and the many stories he told
are engraved in our hearts
forever.

*In Memory of Lester Ward Sr. 1898-1981 RIP

Old Memories

Old memories peer up

at me through dusty faces

as I look through old boxes

I see

Grandpa's old suspenders and

Grandma's old collars of lace

Faces covered in dust look from

their metal frames covered

in rust

Old memories come back to me

to remember days that used

to be.

Christmas Is

Christmas Is
for families
the young and the old
the time when the story
of Christ's birth is told

It's the season of Love, Hope and Joy

the delight of a child when

he sees his new toy

its bright lights on a tree

a wreath on the door

its saying

MERRY CHRISTMAS

but meaning

much more.

I Remember

I remember the days when
we were little and had
our houses by the trees
tree stumps were our tables
and patches of flowers our beds
acorns, leaves and pretty
flat stones our dishes
yes remember when we
would play for hours
making a new table cloth out
of leaves or trying a new
recipe with flowers
but like many houses we
lived in we moved to the
modern world of real big houses
with real dishes of china and
tablecloths made out of fabric
all that stands now are two tree stumps
a few patches of flowers and
the memory of days long ago

The Lady in the River

The lady in the river

watches and waits

for all to come

seeing and hearing their voices

brings a smile to her face

one that has seen many

come to her land

The lady in the river

stands so serene

while the world watches

as she has for centuries

giving a way for those

seeking a new life

in a new land

Hope.

While You Were Sleeping

While you were sleeping
God created the Heavens
and the Earth
While you were sleeping
God gave all life
While you were sleeping
He gave His only son
While you were sleeping
His son healed the blind
and fed two thousand fish
While you were sleeping
His son Jesus was cursed at
Spit upon and nailed to a cross
While you were sleeping
He died for your sins
Hung between two thieves
While you were sleeping
He arose and ascended
Into the shy
While you were sleeping
He is waiting for you
To come unto Him
Are you awake yet?

The Sunset

The sunset fades
like old letters
written on crisp blue paper
lined with pale golden creases
its brillant colors like lines
of words written in different
colors of ink
blurred from endless readings.

In Remembrance

Silent still

the flag rises

in Salute

to the men of wars

long ago

We remember

the men who became soldiers

to protect the land

they are a special band

May we never forget

white stones mark

all that is left

in Remembrance.

Missing You

Missing you
muse
memories nosy around
seeking a place
to visit today
lost between
the pages
of another time
another place
another face
dare we see
through eyes
that cast a shadow
looking into a heart
trying to find all
the pieces.
making it whole
Hope.

A Mother's Love

A Mother's Love
embraces our heart
like no other
Even years later
when she is no longer
here physically
her spirit lingers still....
we feel her in a
hug from her granddaughter
we hear her in the laughter
that escapes our lips
Her touch is everywhere
her love is never ending
because it has made us
the mothers we are
the person we have become
we are strong because of her
lessons learned we make our own
future because of the yesterdays we had
Always remembering "Our Mothers"
and their Love Forever....

Joy

* In Loving Memory Of the Mothers in My Life who have left me in body but are still here in spirit and to those that are still here with me. My Mom, Mary Ellen Chaffman Ward, my grandmother Mary E. Chaffman, My sister Mary Phyllis Ward Guinn and in honor of my aunt Carol Chaffman Tracy. Thanks for always taking care of me.

White Cross

Transcending
into the sky
showing the way
to God
His Power
is real
His Way
is clear
Just Arise
and follow
him
the steps
can be climbed

All invited
to soar
above
he shows
no limits
he is here
for us always
follow the cross
it leads us
HOME

The Shore

I remember the summers of my childhood

At my Grandparents house on the river

Days spent at the shore whether it was

crabbing or enjoying the coolness

of the water as the sun beats its

hot rays upon us

The smell and taste of honeysuckle

as we suck the flowers when we race by them to see who

could get to the water first

My cousins and my sister and I

went to sleep on high beds

and had to run to the outhouse

trying to escape the mosquitoes

that tried to bite us

Those were the days of eating crabs,

corn on the cob

watermelon and peaches

watching the bonfire

sizzle to flame and being told

not to get too close

roasting hotdogs and marshmallows

Climbing our cousin tree

and wishing

we could stay forever

At The Shore.

* In Memory of my grandparents, Edward and Mary Ellen
Chaffman and their house at the river. RIP.

Everything Has A Home

Making my way along the footprints

of my soul choices to make feelings unknown

trying to find the path to take

map shows no way to escape

the emotions I feel deep inside my heart

the very essence of it

shattered even still

trying to put the pieces back together

trying to do it on my own

not willing to ask for help believing it

will make me weak rather than strong

which I know I am only in the moments

that are few and far between that I see the shadows

drifting by trying to take pieces of me.

grabbing them back bit by bit

I know I can make it as long as everything fits

For everything has a home even me.

Kitty Cat Pounce

A jump A pounce

happy cat abounds

leaping learning

furry fun

turning around

figuring it out

what can I do

kitty cat pounce

happy cat here

leaping love

for sure

in all its midst

kitty cat pounce

Fun

Breeze Song

I listen to your breezes

singing me a song

of a Winter day turned Spring

your tune embraces me

in an upbeat swirl

that leaves me breathless

Suddenly the music changes

to a sad song of a Winter day

you leave me cold and outcast

and I wonder will I hear your

Song again Come Spring

Raindrops

Raindrops pouring down
from the sky
touching the earth
with its fingers
like teardrops
from a human eye
water from a faucet
crystal clear stones
shadowing the world
with water.

Mountain Song

I listen to the music

of the mountains

singing me a song

of crisp Autumn nights

that leaves their peaks

Breathless

While the hills holler out

a slow flowing tune of

many loves lost

The mountains sing a

sweet strumming song

of ancient tale

so long ago

their tune lifts my spirits

and leaves me lost in the

beauty of the song

My Beloved Albion

My Beloved Albion
oh how I dream to see
your flowing River Thames
and Lands of such majesty
so many places
Big Ben and St. Paul's
so much to do
Walk by the Thames at sunset
watch the changing of
the Guards
My Beloved Albion
Land of dreams come true
one day I will be there
with You.
My Beloved England

Prisoner of Snow

I am a prisoner of snow

I sit by a window

closed in by the whiteness

that surrounds me

cold whiteness falls

silently threatens

my freedom

it surrounds me like

cold steel bars

and leaves me alone

in my world of white

This Lonesome Day

Sun beamed shadows

across the grass

they come to visit me

this lonesome day

I watch them dance

jump and skip

with joyful glee

if only they could

talk to me

this lonesome day

Through the Eyes of Fall

I see you running

through my leaves

my leaves

so crisp and golden brown

like you

so fresh and your hair

blown and free

I see you picking up

my pine combs

its sharp edges

jabbed your fingers

I see a smile linger

on your face

as you watch my leaves fall

and let my breezes

embrace you

Dusty Black

Strikes his face
down deep in
a hot hole
Earth packs around his back
down and under all around
million dollar money
they never see trying
to survive

Black holes
living by a light
not much to see
black hole above below
all around me
Coal Miner's life
looking through
black dusted lens
leads his way out
Alive

Jesus Christ

Away in a manger

on a long ago night

a star in the sky

a beautiful sight

for Jesus our Lord

was born on that night

a small boy eyes full of love

they never did know how much

he knew of the gifts of above

many years later healing the blind

full of such power

he is so divine

they didn't believe

they didn't care

but that doesn't mean

he isn't there

nailed on a cross thorns on his head

they spit in his face

but he died for all race

three days later

he arose and ascend far above the sky

he never said goodbye

for he is coming back to take us

to the place where he said

there ye shall be also

he's our savior our lord king of the highest throne

he is there he will be back again

until then believe and ye shall receive

Amen

Hope's Road

Hope

makes the heart beat more

sends a burst of sunshine

to an overcast day

travelling past us

not sure of the way

to its designation

the map is unclear

when travelling Life's roads

best not to travel alone

for you may run into dangers

traps all around best to

stay clear upon

steady ground the mind

shows the way there if

the heart will stay strong

one day you will get there

really never alone.

to be.

Heart Beats

Listens to the minutes
ticking by in a moment
of time catches us
briefly
walking through the mists
watching shadows jump and skip
feeling the hug of the wind
sending us soaring through
memories moments passing by
too soon
wishing for yesterdays
in the hold of today cherishing
all that we know and have
embracing all.
the miracle of a soul when a
heart lost Love
hears its beat
once more.

Life's Echo

Life's Echo soars
trying to find its way
through confused clouds
passing roadblocks
its journey never really
knowing which way to go
all in the knowing of the heart
seeking to find a home
and Love abounds
Leads the way.

Melody's Song

Moment of Hesitation
breathe
listen to the moments
speaking whispers
between the silences
unsure minutes pass
the clock chimes
its melody's song
while we wait
still.

Heart Left Too Long

The heart has no understanding
it only knows what it feels
between pulses and beats
it comes alive
for years it kept itself
locked and bolted fragile as it is
many tried to get through
doors so strong but inside
shattered pieces like panes
of glass crushed beyond
repair soul untouched
a stillness no one knows
ghost shadows listen
to its beats and pulses
coming alive bearly
striking breathing in
strange feelings
left untouched
too long

Life's Not Easy

Life doesn't make it easy
the road feels unpaved
not sure which way to go
or even how to escape
life's traffic
I do not have the answer
I don't have a map
or even a plan of attack
but one thing I sure of
God knows it all
has showed me many times
the road I am to travel
my hope in him
in times of destress
makes my days better
when I know he always there
guiding showing helping me
find the way to go
if only we remember
he is the greatest one
to know...

Uncontained Emotions

Soar and fly lifting their wings
In a cloudless sky
never knowing where to go
or even what to do
feel uncontrolled
lost tossed aside
listening to nothing
just trying to find a way
in hopes of a calmer day
Rest

Mercy Rings

Does it count
Hope on the horizon
need not believe
jumps up and runs
fast as it can
no love here
no need to bend
unsure emotions
reactions unclear
need we go further
stop where we are at
felt good for a moment
need I say more
questions abound
meet me at the door
shut and locked so many times
double bolt too so many times
need I open the door
all flows out or in
need I say more
wait and see

is that knock
really for me
a test in time
no idea on the score
Do I want more
dare I enjoy
Hope in the moment
or lock bolt
once more
that never knowing
door of my heart.

Mary Did You Really Know?

Mary did you really know
the baby you had
would be nailed to a cross
on day
Did you really know
the pain he felt or the
job he had to do
Sent here to save a world of ungrateful people
in a time when know one saw
who he really was
a human man pain and hurt
crushed beyond it all
to heal to believe to show
us the way to a heart that never stopped
loving us
Mary what was it like to see
your son dying on a cross
knowing it was for you and all
he died
the hope of the world on his shoulder
throughout eternity He truly gave his life
for You and Me

Love Hope Forgiveness

Love Hope Forgiveness
goes hand in hand
no regrets if
you allow in
memories of yesterday
flows out Hope seeps
slowly forgiveness burns
the never ceasing light
to a new horizon
heaven bound passion
chances taken the luck
of the heart mind fights
a never ending battle
there goes the heart
lost a beat once more
daring to believe
again.

Summer's Sunset and God's Fireworks

Tiny stars scatter
across the sky
as the moon comes up in
a bright white ball
colors so brilliant fade
we gash at the beauty
as we watch
God's fireworks on display

A Galaxy Somewhere

.In a galaxy somewhere
I seek life in a moment
in time
the clock ticks
other times
in places unknown to me
trying to find my way
in unfamiliar territories
without a map
I seek I live and learn
nothing comes easy
in this galaxy somewhere.

* Not a StarW fan this is done for a different reason.

The Tides Shifts

In a moment
the tides can shift
when we least expect it
it can wash us back
away from its fury
or gentle caress
depending on the way
we take it
in its movements
it can change everything
whether we like it or not
our tides can shift all
never knowing when,
where it can happen
life in its rolling tides
can send us away or make us
embrace its midst
hugging the shore
we can seize its moments
carefully watching
our tides shift
once more.

My Poetry Machine

Poof

the words take me off

to another time and place

to people and memories

I wish to visit

poof sends me soaring

distance is no limit

as sounds and feelings soar

to somewhere beyond

my imagination dreams unlashed

fly through skies unlimited

words jump around trying to find

their place

on this trip in my

poetry machine

poof

travels

once more.

Joy

69

Vader, Black Cat Kitty

Black is the night lit only
by the moon
shadows abound
slick and quick
eyes shine bright
black and smooth
kitty cat hunt
as creatures of the night
whish by
Vader.

Bella Girlz Davis RIP

Bella came to us

not a dog I would ever choose

but she's not mine

and the choice was hers and MC

She lived outside a fence

hooked to a chain

saw my daughter

and big chocolate brown eyes

fell in love

she looked for her everyday

never knowing when she would come

some days never at all

but then one day

she came and took her in a car

riding she was

so excited Bella learned

her new home had a large backyard

never had to be hooked up again

she ran and jumped and played

with glee as if to say Hey look

at Me!

Part Border/German she looks as if to often say

I am just so happy to be here!!!

Home At Last

RIP 2008-2017

Love is

Love is Red
it sounds like a soft voice
it smells like the sweetest rose
it tastes like honey
Love feels like a hug.

Snoopy

He's long but short with big
friendly eyes
He runs like a horse but looks a hound
He's there to say hey Snoop to
He's there to say Come on bud
He's even there to talk to
if you don't need one to talk back
He acts as if he understands
and lets his wet tongue show it
He to me is the best dog ever
and I ought to know it!
RIP Snoopy 1981- 1992

Mom, I Remember

Mom, I remember
the roses in your garden
their colors red,pink and yellow
I remember your walk, your talk
though your voice
seems distant to me now
I never forgotten
the way you looked
I see you in my eyes,
I hear your words coming out of me
the mother of long ago lives on
in me the daughter today
and now the grand daughter too
I remember most of all the memories
of yesterday living on today.

Joy

* this poem is old and new coming together many years ago
then added to today, RIP Mary Ellen Chaffman Ward 1933-1973

The Things I Love

The smell of Spring as it gently and softly
awakens the sleeping world
The freedom I have as I run across the field
toward the laughter of voices
the smile on a baby's face and
the whisper of a voice as
it says good night
the beauty of the mountains and the
rushing sound of a brook
the smell of meat cooking and the
beautiful sounds of Home
The things I Love are precious
like little tiny stones that glitter
in the sunlight
the dawn of the day and the stillness
of the night
The smell of rain and the beautiful
sounds of LIFE.

Sunshine
Bright yellow rays
of cheer crossed
her face made into a smile
as her heart warms
the whole Earth.

Love's Melody
Singing softly through
the gloom
the only light is the moon
I let my thoughts wonder through
the lonely streets
wondering if I shall
ever meet the one
who sings Love's melody.

I used to be a scrubby shrub
but now I am a great big tree
in full bloom.

Love bursts like firecrackers
tastes like honey
smells like a rose
feels like a hug.

Love Is Sonnet

Love is the eyes that shines through tears

Love is the tongue that speaks so sweet

Love is the heart that opens ears

Love is the face that is warm with heat

Love is the eyes that tell me you care

Love is the arm that holds me anywhere

Love is solid but often tears

So every Love with torn holes is bare

For the heart and mind are indeed a pair

cause they ease discomfort and the pain

Why then shall I forget my needs

to show my love to others in deeds.

Glimpse of Heaven

I saw a glimpse of heaven today
in angels unaware
the light of a thousand lights
lit up God's world
Beautiful
music from the voices
of angels embrace
my soul
Priceless
The love of God sends me
soaring beyond anything
reachable
His power is all that
I need makes
everything possible
and nothing
Impossible.

My Mother Went Away Today

My mother went away today
I really don't know why
I guess God needed her
more than I
I really don't know why
maybe he liked the way
she looked when
her glasses fell down her nose
when she read a book
I really don't understand why
maybe he liked the way she
cared for me
or how she listened to my prayers
I really don't understand why
I remember those prayers
Now I lay me down to sleep
why God?

I pray the lord my soul to keep

why her there were plenty of others

If I shall die before I wake

No!

there was no one like her

I pray the lord my soul to take

Why God?

I don't think I will ever understand

God bless

I guess you know what's best

Mommy!

A Star in the sky

what a beautiful sight

for Jesus Our Lord

was born on this night.

Ballad of a City, Country Kid

Born in the city raised by the sea

sidewalks, cars and the Chesapeake bay

lived in my land

but it was a true part of me even if

it did sound like a

big instrumental band

yes I am a city kid a city kid am I

lived in a house my daddy bought

sat on my daddy's knee it didn't matter

what they thought the city life is a

part of me

moved away from that city town to a

place that's country as can be

not that I like this southern town

but it too has become apart of me

Now I am a country kid A country kid I am

lived in a house my daddy built sat

in my daddy's chair it didn't matter

what they think the country life is

a part of me

oh I sure the city remembers me

the streets, the cars the Chesapeake Bay

and how they were a true part of me

I still part city kid but a country kid I am

the city still apart of me but now I am

COUNTRY BOUND.!

Memory of Time

In the hills of tomorrow

in the shadows of today

I await for you but

you never came this way

your face is just a memory

of times of yesterday

Broken Dreams

She finds her dreams

all broken

where she had cast them aside

only to find them hard to fix

and battered over time

she tried to fix them

and make them new

but it only makes her

sad and blue

to know that dreams

that once could come true

now are of no use to her

so she packs them away

and hopes once more

for brighter days

when all that she dreams

comes true.

"Cat"

She came and embraced
our lives
all ninety plus pounds
made her presence known
No matter where she was
she was true blue
never changing
always knowing
"Cat"

She had a huge heart
one who gave all
no matter what
always there for you
never ceasing on her love
the pictures on the walls
were the memories in
her soul
her family, her babies
were always her
cherished treasures
Even now as they live on
as she would
through Life's continued chain.

* In Memory of my mother in law who would never be ex to me
RIP Dora Catherine Ivey Davis 1944-1999.

Is It Too Late

Is it too late to capture

a sun beam in my hand

wish upon a star

Listen to the wind capture

a leaf in its grasp

Am I too late to see

the beauty in a sunrise

colors so brilliant

they hurt my eyes

see the power of a bird

as it takes to flight

and then see its fragile legs

gather grass to build

its nest

Is it too late to see the

wonder of the sea

The glorious height

of the mountains

to capture it all in

a moment of time

daring it to stay the same

forever or

is it too late to even

begin

to Hope.

Its 2am

Its 2am

wide awake ramblings

of yesterdays tomorrows

ancestors

long ago

a poem a thought

a prayer

enters my endless file of

brain messages

in this 2am hour

of night

that thinks its daytime

another moment

in time

when sleep doesn't enter

and thinking never stops

yet.

In Memory of "Nana"

Like a butterfly
she soared into our life
bringing color and cheer
to our days
She never spoke an
unkind word
Always said her prayers
She was a true lady
she could have been
anyone's grandmother
with a soul that was young
God gave us a beautiful
Angel
who was a joy to know
her love forever embraced
ours
her love will live on
Forever

*In memory of Helen B. Sellers RIP 1929-2010 Romans 8:28

Prism

Prism of color
Catch a rainbow
in my hand
and hold it close
to my soul
its colors so bright
and full of hope
warms my heart and
leaves me smiling
on an otherwise
gloomy day.

Old Soul

Old faces peer back at me

weathered by years gone by

words lost in a jumbled mind

endlessly trying to escape

a tired soul.

Old Fingers

Old fingers reach
out through the
twilight eve
trying to grab
the last beams
of slanted light
that creeps through
its hands
hoping to stop
another day
from ending
Darkness fold its
grasps like
a blanket
safe and warm
as another day
closes its eyes to sleep.
Good Night.

Goodnight

A Whisper of a Heartbeat

A whisper of a heartbeat

beating strongly

Life Alive and in

the very core of our being

how can we not see life

hear life surrounds us

In our midst a soul

comes into being

tiny fingers, toes

form

Life alive and well

pulsing soars within

us Life hits us

hard but reminds us

within our midst

A Whisper of a heartbeat

Lives Life!! LOVE!

*IN HONOR OF DEAN

Flood

Flood into my soul

God's power and mercy

Flood into my soul

God's everlasting Love

but only God can

release the floodgate

of my soul

that keeps me bound

the power of him

is all I need.

The Real Reason for the Season

The stockings filled with goodies
the tree is aglow
but do we really remember
the real reason for the season
and Christmas as we should know
long time ago
a star in the night sky
led the way
and gave us the first
Christmas Day
a stable awaits
for a birth of a king
one who came
announced only by a few
the ones who really knew
angels who lit up the sky
proclaiming his birth
for you and I
and all as we remember
Our Savior, Our King
Celebrate HIM
Never forget
His Greatest Gift!!
Merry Christmas!!

Our Haven

We seek refuge in this place
where laughter, love and rhyme
happens
words hold hands dance among the flowers
seek and find a place to dream to share
a common bond
Our haven holds us together
hearts bring the distance
closer finding our paths
a little more near among
the flowers thorns and tree
we embrace our inner soul
powerful it is and for a little while
we make the world a little better
our dreams are the same to share a word
make a verse a prayer a poem a song
a piece of writing that lifts from our soul
a its all right in our world and we want to share it
with yours.
Embrace the moment
live, love and laugh
family of Poetry Alliance
Rock On

* www.poetryandpublishing.com

Love Hummm

Love can come

in many tones

of red

pretty petals

slightly damp with dew

crushing hearts bleed red

heartbroken soul

cries tears no longer clear

bubbling bursting sobs

run red rivers

in the cold of the night

mourning breaks

scarlet sunrise leaves

streaks of red across the sky

pounding heart beats still

LOVE gone wrong

runs RED...

Family Love

You are the creation
of a thousand loves
passed down through
many generations
ancestors laughed and lived
through you
making you who you are many
loves and lives later
living on today
in yesterday's moments
Love lives on
Family...

Pain

Piercing, actions,

invade

no one

wishing is a song

that sings no tune

Love loops around us

nevermore to be

a fairy in a magic land

enchantment does she see

all because a word

made a sentence

a rhyme came to be

surely meant for me

hoping it will free me

from piercing pain actions

that invade no one

but ME

 Joy

Anger

thorns jab our fingers

anger pounds in our heart

blood seeps out

flowing as if to stop

our hope

Forgiveness

we feel none

anger plenty

peace any to find

not any day

soon I guess still

trying to find

the way to cross

the gap that

lies in the way

today.

A Mom's Christmas Memory

As I look back on the memory

of Christmas past today

I remember my Mom

the one who made the magic

happen in spite of the fact

she also told me there was no Santa but

she gave me the memories like

helping me look up

publishers in the phonebook

on Christmas eve when I wrote my first "book"

she believed in Me and

gave me a lifetime of

memories like big appliance boxes covered in shiny

paper filled to the top with presents

lighting the Advent Candles and

making sure

I had a little tree in my room

she lives on today in me with my daughter her namesake

as she lights the candles, has her own tree and

is thrilled with all her presents under the tree

but she also enjoys the magic of Santa

longer than I did

as I remember my mom's memories reach out

to embrace me once more

this Christmas Day.

Gracie/Grayce

Bundle of gray

lived a life full of wonder

contentment and peace

Did what she wanted

pretty much

the queen of the house

always got her way

but others cared more

adored those

she missed

but accepted

what she didn't understand

Live a Life full

a bundle of gray

that saw more

with her eyes

than anybody realized

a soul that knew

who

she loved

after all

and just

put up with the rest of us

even to the end.

Rest in Peace

Gray Cat Kitty

We love You

Good night...

*In memory of Gracie/Grayce 2001-2013 RIP

Painter of Darkness

A river of black

flows from my brush

as I a painter

of darkness

paints another night

shadows jump around me

as I try to bring to life

the essence of darkness

upon a canvas

so white.

The Battle

I feel the battle

inside bursting

forth like a volcano

sending its hot lava

everywhere

words sharp like swords

feeling the pain

inflict the heart

trying to find a way

to make it through

the war zone

wishing for a end

waiting for a beginning

seeking peace...

Thankful

For times spent
together
with those we love
memories of days
long ago
flood our thoughts
dinners made special
by grandmothers
who live on
through us
Thankful
for all we have
and even for
all we lost
for without
pain
we could never
be grateful
thankful
to God
who knows
all and is still
in our midst
on this our day
of Thanks...

Unfair

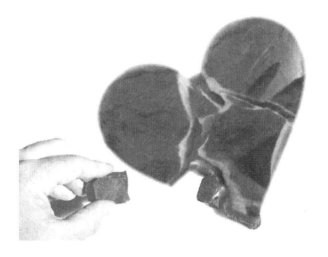

the unfairness of life
comes stomping in
making a mess
all over the place
leaving everything astray
torned and battered
trying to pick up
the pieces again
doesn't get any
easier
even now...

Like Father Like Son

Years past
has made his face
tired and creased
harden
trying to live
young
in a old body
An old man
trying to get
into heaven
with past deeds
catching up
with him
In his eyes
nothing learned
only mistakes
made as he
tries to
move on
a old man
living in a
lifeless soul...

...

Defeated

airless balloon

drifting to earth

nothing left but the hope

that a little breeze will blow

to lift it soaring again

with God all things

are possible

even when

we feel defeated

just have to

believe and hope

again.

Scars of life

He wore scars

for us

felt them in his hands

on his back

everywhere

by doing so he died

a senseless death

for us

leaving

too soon

saving us

forever...

The Fight

I feel the sword cut

into me

its sharp edges

slice me

like the bitter words

slapping my soul

leaving me shocked

at their meaning

I seek comfort

in the night

but even the darkness

gives nothing to me

lying in pain heart and soul

Is the battle over yet

or is the Fight continuing on...

Blue

Blue is the color
of the sky
feels crisp and cool
to touch
like blueberries
ready to eat

Christ is Here

Christ is here
in presents
in songs
in making a
Happy day
Christ is here
its Christmas
His birthday
today.

* I think this is my oldest poem, written when I was 7 or 8 years old.

Night Wishes

As she sits in the coolness

of the sunset as

another day closes its

eyes to sleep

even as the silence embraces

the night

All is not still in her soul

as it feels the noise of the darkness

the whispers, the groans

that never cease to be

restless is the night

Looking In

Look within
my soul
its feelings
pulsing
pushing their way
around my heart
not knowing
which one needs
to be released
within its close
encounters
one bursts
out
whirling its way
soaring like an
bird free
from all dangers
that impacted
its home
looking within
flying out
finally free...

Shattered

feelings shattering
like glass
beneath my feet
but within my heart
that feels the pain
tears fall
like raindrops
trying to wash away the pain
that once again
lays broken
into a thousand pieces
impossible to fix
again.

In Memory of Maya Angelo

She called herself a poet

in love with the "Music of Language"

the sound of words coming

alive with a majestic voice

she sung their words

made them shout

as her life truly was

with the power she

had inside

a soul bursting to make

known all that she was and

still is today

in the hearts of everyone she

met and everyone she embraced

her love of words and the power

that made them come alive

embracing life to the fullest

we will never forget

"The Pulse"

she was in our lives

The "Amazing Peace"

she brought to so many

she will live on forever

in our hearts and soul.

- RIP Dr. Maya Angeleo

Fragments

Life leaves fragments scattered
trying to catch them all
as we straggle to grab
and keep up
Life sends us
soaring
as we try to grab
all the pieces
hoping to
keep them together
today.

Loss

Feels like a cold wind
chilling our bones
a heartbeat slowed
a teardrop falling
uncertain feelings flowing
through our thoughts
leaving us wounded
on the battlefield
of life
Loss

Through the Eyes of Winter

I see you running through my snow
its icy fingers reaching out to grab you
cold breezes leaves your face frozen and red
I see you picking up my snow
making a snowball
I watch you throw it through
the air your laughter soars
as my snow falls all around
leaving the world
covered in white.
embracing you
Cold...

Red

RED

is the color

of your heart

when you like

someone

RED is blood

when you cut yourself

RED is koolaid

you drink

cool on a hot

summer day

RED is a cherry

Juicy sweet

RED is a fire truck

blazing by……

*Another of Mary-Catherine's color poems

Love's Melody

Singing softly through

the gloom

the only light

is the moon

I let my thoughts wander

through the lonely street

wondering if

I shall

ever meet

the one

that sings love's melody.

A Chance

Life brings
a chance
our way
embracing
the choice
of the moment
not knowing what
it is here for
fluttering
through our thoughts
waiting to land
caught
unaware
seizes our day
making anything
possible
and nothing
impossible

Kate

She walks
to meet her prince
in sheer beauty
All eyes upon her
Magic in the moment
as she embraces all
that is to be
A princess in the making
everlasting love
sharing her day
with so many
but most of all
her prince now
Everlasting Love
As they sealed
their Love
Forever
William

.Changes

My soul feels
the changes
in the wind
as the leaves fly
through the crisp
cool air
sending my spirit
soaring
not knowing where
they will land
uncertain is their
future like mine
will they be crushed
or sent soaring
again on
a hope of
another day
life.

Storm

Storm clouds gather black gray
releases its rafe on another day
silence fills the air
but only for a second
suddenly a roar bursts the moment
leaving everything
crushed and distroyed
and nothing the same
again
Tornado

Zerrissenheit
(Brokeness)

Shattered into a
thousand pieces
zerrissenheit
of my heart
lying in its
scattered form
the torn to pieces
land of my soul
daring
zerrissenheit
the pieces
to come back
together
is there really
enough glue
to hold it
all in place
do I even dare
to try
Zerrissenheit
lies the heartbreak
of it all
nevermore.

Trust

Its sharp edges
rub against my fingers
cuts into my heart
chipped pieces
leaves me
powerless
to no one
trust
only in my God
for within him
I know
someday
my heart will heal
and his power
will restore
me
Trust

Joy

Solitude

Life gives us
moments of solitude
from the everyday noise
life brings
it allows us to
escape like
when we were children
hiding under the covers
wishing all the monsters
would go away making
our world safe and secure
and quiet
if only for a moment
Rest.

God's Power Answered Prayers

Gods power in a strange land

seeks out to those laid helpless

words spoken in a prayer

from the lips of strangers

always seeking the power

in need hoping to help

those that seek

prayers

that heals body

and soul God never forgets

his children as they hope

for their answered prayers

Praise for the father

Amen

Time Waits for No One

as it soars through

our days

never saying

goodbye

time waits for no one

it reaches out and grabs

whatever it sees

that makes life

move forward

time waits for no one

because in its doing

we are already

there

Moment of Time

In the silence

of the moment

Time waits for no one

it soars through the day

leaving its presence

everywhere

Time waits for no one

as we only have this minute

that seizes the day

tomorrow is only a wish

that hasn't been made

in this moment of Time

Tick Tock...

New Year

The clock strikes twelve

a ball falls

New Year begins

are we ready

a blank page

Time and days

go by

clean fresh start

dare we to hope

for closure of

the past

dare we believe

a finish chapter

a new one begins

again

Man with a Thousand Faces
(Part1)

Man with a thousand faces

searching

for what he knows not

the emotions he feels

leaves a burden

too heavy to carry about

He looks to the heavens above

the stars shine bright

this night

They hold no answers for him

His hope has run dry.

he wanders on

thinking maybe

he will find the answers

tomorrow

as another day ends...

Man with a Thousand Faces

(Part2)

Man with a thousand faces

His walks have taken

him everywhere

his journey far from complete

many faces he has seen

many voices he has heard

speak to him in sadness and

mostly confusion

He has felt it all

his heart knows all the emotions

His steps continue on

to where he knows not

forever searching

for a peace

he has not found

for a man with a thousand faces shows no one

his soul for its far too broken

for anyone to understand or fix

he continues on his journey

where he hopes will be

some sort of way that

would be better

than where he is at

alone

Man with a Thousand Faces
(Part3)

Man with a thousand faces
looks down the long dusty road
again searching
for the way to the end or
is it a beginning
he does not know
his face weathered
by time and fate
choices made the journey
not a easy road
the sun blindes his eyes as
a steady rain starts to fall
as water washes over him
he feels refreshed if only
his soul could feel the same
as he continues on
trying to find rest
in a troubled land..

Man with a Thousand Faces
(Part 4)

Man with a thousand faces
His heart feels heavy
as he walks along
nothing feels right
nothing is right
is there really light
at the end of the tunnel
He is not sure where
the answers are or even
if there are any
life without hope
grace without joy
love in his eyes
the stars are dim
across a black sky
faith without works
how can he believe
and for sure
in what
God.
How can there be
has he forgot about
Me?

Man with a Thousand Faces
(Part 5)

Man with a thousand faces
Around the bend
he walks though
his path seems uncertain
like his life
a journey taken
without a care in the world
for he has nothing
to care about
no love loss
not anyone waiting
by the home fires
for him he could
come and go as he pleases
mostly goes no reason to stay
in one place for long
just another day walking
life's road trying to
find Home
If he can
if there is such
a place
who knows..

Man with a Thousand Faces
(Part 6)

Man with a thousand Faces

Through the years

Life has brought him

many sorrows, loves loss and grief

Throught the years he has celebrated

many victories that only the pleasures

of others have given him

Through the years many times

loneliness has overcome him

the feeling of despair

drains his soul

As he searches for direction

to help him cope a way to go

when know one has the answers

leaving him lost

again.

Man with a Thousand Faces
(Part 7)

Man with a thousand faces
feels the sun on his back
as he searches for a place
to lay his head
drained from walking
the long roads
The emotions of his soul
bursting with pain
as he remembers
past moments in life
that have only brought
him sadness
with no way to escape
and no where to go
he looks to the sky
dark as midnight
and prays
never knowing for sure
what for
but maybe someone
will hear him
as he bears "his cross"
alone...

Man with a Thousand Faces
(Part 8)

Man with a thousand faces
feels as if he is standing on
the edge of nowhere
seeking looking
many roads travelled
each one sends him
to the next place in time
where finding the answers
is not easy in a place
where everyone knows
everything and no one
really knows nothing.
he continues on
trying to figure it
out in a world where
no one listens
to him anyway
He walks alone..
even still.

Time Tick Tock

Time waits for no one
as the hands of
the clock move around
Tick tock
we wait and watch
never enough hours
in a day
always more time needed
do we dare to try
and finish this task
tick tock
Time waits for no one
slowly it moves
through our days
but then again
one day we find
ourselves trying
to push the hands back
tick tock
its moved too fast
and now we need
another minute another hour
another day, month and year
to finish what we started
tick tock
or have enough time
to begin....

Baltimore

In the city of marble steps
With misty waters passing through
The sun creeps over the rooftops
closing in on another day
The noise of city life never stops
That was once a part of me
I journeyed many roads to get
where I am at the choices weren't
mine but I am glad they were made
for the town I am in is much better
for me
growing becoming the person I am
makes life in this town the best choice of all
And the memories of that city will never
cease continuing to live on in my heart
Forever.

Minutes in a life

In my life of 53 years
27856800 minutes have'
past me bye
most of them spent
waiting
The beating of the clock
inside me
ever knowing how long
it will be.
minutes, seconds, turn into
days, months and years
long journey travelled
dusty dirt roads, lead me
forward a mission, a quest
Time goes on
again 1440 minutes later
another day
ends.
adding to Life.
and its continued journey

Grief

Grief is never easy
it sweeps through uninviting
like an ocean wave
whish everything
in its path lost
along the way
leaving nothing
left emptyness
teardrops fall
like water from a faucet
never even stopping
when our heart
overflows from
breaking
life ceases to be
our loss
in death
one day we
will have all
the answers
one day we will
understand why
one day we will
see them again
one day our grief
will be gone
and we will know all
God.

Whirlwind of life

My life feels like a whirlwind

that doesn't know where

its going to land

just keeps being

air bound

not knowing

the damage

it may cause

leaves me holding

my breath

and hoping its

cruel hands

never reach me

not today

not ever.

Dragonfly

Dragonfly flicks
its stained glass window wings
across the flower petals
its colors blue and green
sends rainbows soaring
on this sunny day
seeking its way it goes
soaring through a sky
lost in its moment
of time.
Beautiful

Friends

The bulldog

 the wolf dog,

a beagle

a terrier

 a wiener dog

border collie

such a unusual group
make up many honorable traits
each gives their all in different ways
making all days interesting

they guide, they seek, they watch
everything each has its own ways
making life all the more fun
to smile to laugh to know
what to do and say and be.
always there for me.
Getting us all wherever
we need to be
together

Carol   Dale   Debbie   Dena   Joy   Mary-Catherine

* In honor of my friends, Carol, Dena, Debbie, Dale
and Mary-Catherine always looking out for me.

"Thanks"

Crying Child Island

In an island mist

Sounds of wails

Like a crying child

Lost Cougar

Trails and follows

Listens

As a pulsing heartbeat races

Seeking its prey

Unaware of the dangers abound

And a fate unknown...

Only when the Ancestral cries are heeded

through the growing dawn mists

what will be your fate is as it has been.

For many generations

Even before you arrived

I await your return

Wisdom granted for those that seek

Here...

As the island calls you to come

Home....

Roaming the land where water rules

Seeking food needing sleep

The hunt of prey is

Never ending

Trying to survive

Another day

Luck of chance

As daylight breaks

The scent is near

Too tired to follow

But the need is greater

Once again

The quest continues

Instinct guides you

Just as it has guided each

From your Bloodline

A newness captures your

Attention

The air is warm today

Prey is cautious

This land is protection

For the Bloodline's newest born

They thrive only if they also heed

Ancestral Wisdom

Movement

Hunger

The chase

A scream

Silence

Sounds of the insects resumes

Calls the all-clear

Prey is relieved

All but one....

Pacing her steps

She searches

The island

The need of sleep

Now greater

Than any prey

Finding her way

Into a new day

In need of sleep

Restless she is

Time will tell

When and where

The hunt

Begins again

Once more

A scent of danger

Men have invaded this swamp

Cougar must evade them to save her cub

They hear the scream of the cougar's dying prey

As silent as the swamp will allow

The hunters stalk

One teaches his son the hunter's moves

Their smell invades the cougar's senses

Danger finds no sleep

She must protect her child

Cougar's Ancestor's stalk her mind

They will seek and protect their youngest life

Gun is shouldered

A shot

A death

Mother's blood is spilled

Just as she hears

Her Crying Child

153

One who will grow to hunt this hunter's young

The Ancestors will wait

As their youngest cub

survives thrives hunts and pounces

The sunset comes too soon

The cycle in this swamp island continues...

As does Life's Forever Chain...

154

© Joy Ward Davis and Dena M Ferrari

Fund Raising

http://www.apfpublisher.com/funds.html

Fund Raising Anthology

http://www.apfpublisher.com/funds.html